A NUMBER OF DRAGONS

A NUMBER OF DRAGONS

WRITTEN AND ILLUSTRATED BY
LOREEN LEEDY

HOLIDAY HOUSE · NEW YORK

Library of Congress Cataloging in Publication Data

Leedy, Loreen.
    A number of dragons.

    SUMMARY: Introduces the numbers one through ten as a
group of young dragons play together and alone.
    1. Children's stories, American. [1. Counting.
2. Stories in rhyme. 3. Dragons—Fiction] I. Title.
PZ8.3.L4995Nu 1985   [E]   85-730
ISBN 0-8234-0568-0

To OLIVIER, with love and thanks

Ma dragon yells, "Go out and play!"
Ten little dragons rush to obey,

Nine little dragons kick a big ball,

Eight little dragons climb over a wall,

Seven little dragons dangle in trees,

Six little dragons tease some bees,

5

Five little dragons run from a toad,

Four little dragons dance on a road,

Three little dragons crawl up a log,

Two little dragons creep through a fog,

One little dragon digs up a bone,

He wants it for his very own,

All the dragons are out of sight,
It's getting dark—it's almost night,

One little dragon is all alone,

One little dragon buries the bone,

Two little dragons trot through the fog,

Three little dragons slide down the log,

Four little dragons dash up the road,

Five little dragons chase after the toad,

Six little dragons fly faster than bees,

Seven little dragons swing in the trees,

Eight little dragons leap over the wall,

Nine little dragons roll the big ball,

Ten little dragons are home once more,
Ten little dragons begin to snore.